Essential
MEXICAN
COOKERY

Essential
MEXICAN
COOKERY

CHANCELLOR
PRESS

First published in Great Britain in 1994 by Chancellor Press
an imprint of Reed Consumer Books Limited
Michelin House, 81 Fulham Road, London SW3 6RB
and Auckland, Melbourne, Singapore and Toronto

Designed and produced by SP Creative Design
Linden House, Kings Road, Bury St Edmunds, Suffolk, England
Editor and writer: Heather Thomas
Art Director: Al Rockall
Designer: Rolando Ugolini

Copyright © 1994 Reed International Books Limited

ISBN 1 85152 663 3

A CIP catalogue record for this book is available from the
British Library

Printed in Spain by Cayfosa, Barcelona.

Acknowledgements

Special photography: Graham Kirk
Step-by-step photography: GGS Photographics, Norwich
Food preparation: Gillian MacLaurin and Dawn Stock
Styling: Helen Payne
Mexican dishes: Graciella Sanchez and Mexicolore

Notes

1. Standard spoon measurements are used in all recipes.
1 tablespoon = one 15ml spoon
1 teaspoon = one 5ml spoon

2. Both imperial and metric measurements have been
given in all recipes. Use one set of measurements
only and not a mixture of both.

3. Eggs should be size 3 unless otherwise stated.

4. Milk should be full fat unless otherwise stated.

5. Fresh herbs should be used unless otherwise stated.
If unavailable, use dried herbs as an alternative, but halve the
quantities stated.

6. Ovens should be preheated to the specified temperature.
If using a fan assisted oven, follow the manufacturer's
instructions for adjusting the time and the temperature.

CONTENTS

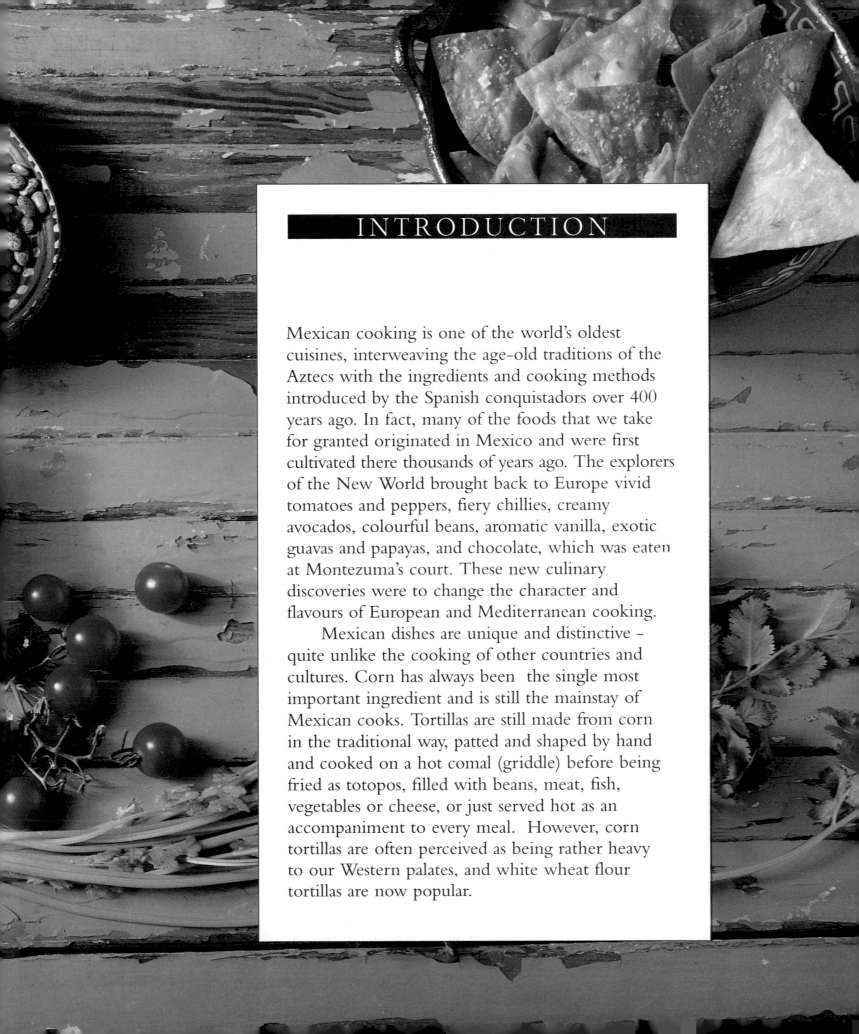

INTRODUCTION

Mexican cooking is one of the world's oldest cuisines, interweaving the age-old traditions of the Aztecs with the ingredients and cooking methods introduced by the Spanish conquistadors over 400 years ago. In fact, many of the foods that we take for granted originated in Mexico and were first cultivated there thousands of years ago. The explorers of the New World brought back to Europe vivid tomatoes and peppers, fiery chillies, creamy avocados, colourful beans, aromatic vanilla, exotic guavas and papayas, and chocolate, which was eaten at Montezuma's court. These new culinary discoveries were to change the character and flavours of European and Mediterranean cooking.

Mexican dishes are unique and distinctive - quite unlike the cooking of other countries and cultures. Corn has always been the single most important ingredient and is still the mainstay of Mexican cooks. Tortillas are still made from corn in the traditional way, patted and shaped by hand and cooked on a hot comal (griddle) before being fried as totopos, filled with beans, meat, fish, vegetables or cheese, or just served hot as an accompaniment to every meal. However, corn tortillas are often perceived as being rather heavy to our Western palates, and white wheat flour tortillas are now popular.

Avocados

Known to the Aztecs as ahuacatl, avocados have been cultivated in Mexico since 7000BC. They may be rough or smooth skinned and range in colour from green to black. Inside, the delicious flesh is pale green with a creamy, buttery texture. They form the basis of guacamole, the classic avocado sauce which is served with literally everything in Mexico.

Avocados are ripe when they yield slightly when pressed with the fingers. Unripe ones will feel hard and should be placed in a paper bag and left for a few days at room temperature to ripen. Avocados discolour rapidly when they are cut, but brushing with lime or lemon juice will help prevent this.

Beans

These originated in Mexico around 5000BC and have remained a staple of Mexican cookery. Many varieties are used: black, haricot, kidney and pinto beans are all popular, as are chickpeas (garbanzos) which were introduced by the Spanish. The most common way of serving beans is frijoles refritos (refried beans). These are beans which have been cooked and are then mashed and fried in lard. The heavy bean paste is used as a filling for tortillas or served with a meal.

Dried beans are soaked in cold water before using, often overnight, until they swell. They are then drained and cooked in fresh water by boiling for two to three hours in an earthenware pot. It is important that they are checked regularly so that they do not boil dry.

Chillies

The colourful chilli gives Mexican food its flair and fire. Grown in Mexico for 9,000 years, chillies come in many varieties, fresh and dried. The Mexicans are connoisseurs and regard chillies with the same reverence that the French reserve for their wines. Afficionados can distinguish subtle differences in their flavour, degree of hotness and intensity. Although we cannot obtain the wide range of chillies that is available in Mexico, the following ones can be purchased in many other countries.

Fresh chillies

Jalapeño: these are dark green, long, hot and fiery.

Poblano: these are dark green and tapering and as large as a green pepper. They are often stuffed.

Serrano: these small chillies may be green or red. Hot and tapering, they are used for making guacamole.

Note: Take care when handling fresh or dried chillies – the seeds can burn your skin. Wash your hands thoroughly afterwards or wear rubber gloves. Remember the golden rule: the smaller the chilli, the hotter it is.

Dried chillies

Ancho: these are dried poblano chillies. Relatively mild, they are a wrinkled deep, reddish-brown colour.

Chipotle: these brick-red dried jalapeno chillies can be bought dried or canned.

Mulato: these pungent brownish-red chillies are mild to moderate in their heat and intensity.

Note: All dried chillies should be soaked in warm water for at least 30 minutes before using.

Chocolate (cocoa)

Legend has it that Quetzacoatl, the Aztec god of light, taught the Mexicans how to grow cocoa and make chocolate, the sacred drink of the gods. The Aztecs roasted and ground the cocoa beans, and then mixed them with water to make a hot chocolate drink, sweetened with honey and flavoured with vanilla and spices. Only the elite ruling class drank

chocolate, and it is still prepared in the traditional way, by whisking with a carved wooden *molinillo* until it is frothy. Chocolate is also used in some savoury dishes, and it is always added to *mole*, Mexico's most famous dish.

Coriander

This herb is not indigenous to Mexico; it was probably introduced by the Spanish after the conquest. It has become the most favoured herb of Mexican cooks and is used in most savoury dishes. It resembles flat-leaf parsley but has a very distinctive intense flavour and there is no real substitute. Oregano and parsley are also used to flavour dishes as is epazote.

Lard

This is commonly used for frying beans and other foods. Bacon dripping is also popular and oils are seldom favoured. However, you can substitute olive, vegetable or sunflower oils instead.

Salsas

These are sauces which are usually made from chillies and tomatoes and are served with cooked fish, meat, poultry, beans and eggs, or added to tortillas before stuffing. In the West and in Tex-Mex cookery, which is widespread in the United States, hot, fiery salsas are used as dips for *totopos* (fried tortilla chips).

Seviche

This method of 'cooking' raw fish or seafood by marinating it in lime or lemon juice is common in Mexico and throughout Latin America. The fish should be marinated for about three to five hours until it loses its translucence and looks 'cooked'. It is usually eaten as an hors d'oeuvre before the main course.

Tequila

This is the fiery spirit of Mexico, made from the fermented sap of the maguey plant. It is the basis of Margaritas, which are now drunk all over the world. In Mexico, tequila is usually served neat in small glasses, frosted with salt around the rim, embellished only with a slice of fresh lime.

Tomatoes

The Mexicans use red or green (husk) tomatoes. They are used in fresh and cooked sauces and in making guacamole. The little green tomatoes, *tomatillos*, are very popular with a delicate flavour. They are not the same as unripe green tomatoes, but have a loose outer covering. They are available canned outside of Mexico, and may be grown from seed.

Tortillas

These are unique to Mexico and were traditionally made from ground corn husks. Now they are made from *masa harina*, a fine dried corn flour, or from wheat flour. What makes them unusual is that, unlike other breads, they are made from cooked flour as the dried corn has already been boiled, dried and ground to make the instant masa.

The cooked tortillas are stacked up in a basket and wrapped in a cloth to keep them warm before serving with every meal. They are used in a variety of Mexican dishes:

Burritos: stuffed tortilla parcels.
Enchiladas: tortillas dipped in chilli sauce, filled and baked.
Flautas: tortillas rolled tightly into cylinders around a filling and fried.
Quesadillas: tortillas folded over cheese and then fried.
Tacos: tortillas stuffed and rolled into cylinders, eaten soft or fried.
Tostadas: crisp, fried tortillas topped with meat or beans and served with salsa and guacamole.
Totopos: tortillas cut into wedges and fried until crisp and golden. They are sprinkled with coarsely ground salt and may be used as dippers for guacamole or refried beans.

Cooking equipment

In the traditional Mexican kitchen, there are only a few basic cooking utensils.

Cazuelas: together with ollas, these are the earthenware casseroles and claypots used for cooking stews and moles. Rough on the outside, they are glazed and smooth on the inside. Before using for the first time, they must be seasoned. Mexican cooks do this by rubbing them with a clove of garlic and then filling with cold water and a bundle of fresh herbs. The pots are then baked in a moderate oven or simmered on top of the stove for several hours until the water evaporates, leaving the pot dry.

Comal: this is a griddle used for cooking tortillas.

Metate: this is a heavy three-legged stone, made of basalt and used for grinding corn, cocoa and chillies.

Molcajete and tejolote: this heavy mortar and pestle consists of a round volcanic bowl on three legs and a pestle made of black basalt. It is used for grinding chillies and spices.

Tortilla press: although tortillas are traditionally made by hand, patting and slapping them into shape, it is easier to use a cast-iron tortilla press to flatten the dough to a small thin round.

TORTILLAS

Flour tortillas

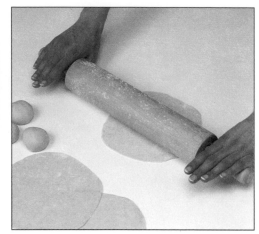

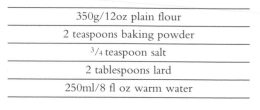

| 350g/12oz plain flour |
| 2 teaspoons baking powder |
| ³/4 teaspoon salt |
| 2 tablespoons lard |
| 250ml/8 fl oz warm water |

1 Sift the flour, baking powder and salt into a large bowl. Cut the lard into tiny pieces and add to the flour. Gradually stir in enough warm water to form a soft dough.

3 Roll a ball of dough out into a round, about 18cm/7 inches in diameter, on a lightly floured surface. Repeat this process with the other balls of dough.

4 Heat an ungreased griddle or cast iron skillet until it is very hot. Put a tortilla on the griddle and cook over moderately high heat until bubbles start to appear. Turn the tortilla over and cook the other side, gently pressing out the bubbles that form, until golden brown. The cooked tortillas should be soft and pliable. Stack them up and keep them warm while you cook the remaining tortillas.

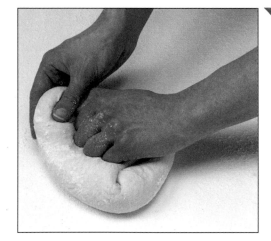

2 Turn the dough out on to a lightly floured surface and knead until smooth and elastic. Divide into 12 small portions and shape each into a ball. Cover with a cloth and leave to rest for 15-20 minutes.

PREPARATION: 30-35 MINUTES
COOKING: 10 MINUTES
SERVES: 6-8

GUACAMOLE

Avocado dip with tortilla chips

2 large ripe avocados
3 tablespoons lemon or lime juice
2 garlic cloves, crushed
40g/1½ oz chopped spring onions
1-2 tablespoons chopped mild green chillies or jalapenos
2 tablespoons chopped fresh coriander
salt and black pepper
125g/4oz skinned, seeded and chopped tomatoes
For the totopos:
8 corn or wheat tortillas
oil for deep frying
sea salt

2 Put the avocado flesh in a mixing bowl with the remaining lemon or lime juice, and mash coarsely. Add the garlic, spring onions, chillies and coriander and some seasoning to taste. Mix in the chopped tomatoes. Cover the bowl and place in the refrigerator for at least 1 hour.

1 Cut the avocados in half, and carefully remove the peel and stones. Scoop out the flesh and sprinkle with a little of the lemon or lime juice to prevent it discolouring.

PREPARATION: 15 MINUTES +
1 HOUR CHILLING
COOKING: 5 MINUTES
SERVES: 6

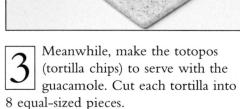

3 Meanwhile, make the totopos (tortilla chips) to serve with the guacamole. Cut each tortilla into 8 equal-sized pieces.

4 Deep fry the tortillas in hot oil until they are crisp and golden. Drain on absorbent kitchen paper and sprinkle with a little sea salt. Serve with the guacamole.

NACHOS

Spicy tortilla chips with cheese

1. Make the chilli sauce: heat the oil in a small saucepan and sauté the onion and garlic until soft and golden, stirring occasionally.

2. Add the tomatoes, chillies, oregano, cumin and seasoning. Bring to the boil and then reduce the heat and simmer gently for 15 minutes, or until the chilli sauce is thickened and reduced.

3. Arrange the tortilla chips on a large ovenproof dish or plate and then carefully spoon the chilli sauce over the top of them.

2 tablespoons oil	
1 onion, chopped	
2 garlic cloves, crushed	
4 large tomatoes, skinned and chopped	
175g/6oz canned jalapeno chillies or 2 fresh red chillies, seeded and chopped	
pinch of dried oregano	
pinch of ground cumin	
salt and pepper	
250g/8oz tortilla chips (see page 12)	
125g/4oz grated cheese	
125ml/4 fl oz sour cream	
125ml/4 fl oz guacamole	

To garnish:

diced onion and tomato

4. Sprinkle with grated cheese and cook in a preheated oven at 180°C/350°F/Gas Mark 4 until the cheese melts and starts to bubble. Serve the nachos with the sour cream and guacamole, garnished with diced onion and tomato.

PREPARATION: 30 MINUTES
COOKING: 10 MINUTES
SERVES: 4-6

QUESADILLAS
Cheese-stuffed tortillas

1 Put the tortillas on a board and divide the refried bean mixture between them, putting a spoonful of mixture on half of each tortilla and leaving a little space around the edge of the loaded side.

2 Put a little grated cheese and some sliced Mozzarella on top of the refried beans, and then a few slices of chilli. Fold the tortilla over the top of the filling.

3 Press the edges of each folded tortilla firmly together between your fingertips. It helps if the tortillas are soft and quite damp when you do this. If necessary, secure them with cocktail sticks. Cover the folded tortillas with a damp cloth while you make the remaining quesadillas.

4 Heat some oil in a large pan to a depth of 4cm/1½ inches, and fry the quesadillas, a few at a time, until crisp and golden brown. Remove and drain on absorbent kitchen paper. Serve the quesadillas hot with salsa, guacamole and sour cream.

12 soft wheat or corn tortillas
175g/6oz refried beans (see page 82)
225g/8oz Monterey jack or Cheddar cheese, grated
125g/4oz Mozzarella cheese, cut into strips
4-6 fresh green chillies, seeded and thinly sliced
oil for cooking
To serve:
salsa, guacamole, sour cream

PREPARATION: 15 MINUTES
COOKING: 5-10 MINUTES
SERVES: 4-6

FLAUTAS

Tortilla flutes

400g/14oz refried beans (see page 82)

2 fresh green chillies, chopped

50g/2oz onion, chopped

25g/1oz toasted chopped almonds

2 tablespoons chopped fresh coriander

125g/4oz grated cheese

8 corn or wheat tortillas

oil for frying

To serve:

red chilli sauce (see page 110)

1 avocado, stoned, peeled and sliced

2 Meanwhile, wrap the tortillas in foil and warm in a low oven to soften them. Spoon a little of the refried bean and cheese mixture along the centre of each warmed tortilla.

1 Put the refried beans and chillies in a pan and heat through gently, stirring occasionally so that they do not stick. Mix in the onion, almonds, coriander and cheese.

3 Roll up each tortilla carefully and tightly to form a flute. If necessary, secure with wooden cocktail sticks to prevent them opening during the frying process.

4 Heat the oil, about 2.5cm/1 inch deep, in a heavy frying pan and fry the flautas in batches until they are crisp and lightly browned all over. Drain on some absorbent kitchen paper. Serve the flautas with red chilli sauce and sliced avocado.

PREPARATION: 20 MINUTES
COOKING: 10 MINUTES
SERVES: 4

HUEVOS RANCHEROS

Baked ranch-style eggs

2 onions, finely chopped

3 garlic cloves, crushed

2 red peppers, seeded and chopped

2 fresh red chillies, seeded and chopped

2 tablespoons lard

1 teaspoon dried oregano

1/2 teaspoon ground cumin

salt and pepper

4 large tomatoes, skinned and chopped

125ml/4 fl oz tomato paste

125ml/4 fl oz water or stock

4 eggs

1 tablespoon chopped fresh coriander

1 large avocado, stoned and sliced

2 Add the chopped tomatoes and the tomato paste together with 125ml/4 fl oz water (or stock if wished). Bring to the boil and then reduce the heat and simmer gently until the sauce reduces and thickens.

3 Pour the prepared tomato sauce into a large greased ovenproof dish and then make 4 wells, or indentations, in the tomato sauce with the back of a spoon.

1 Sauté the onions, garlic, peppers and chillies in the lard until soft and golden. Add the oregano, cumin and seasoning to taste. Stir into the onion and pepper mixture and cook for 2 minutes.

4 Carefully break an egg into each well. Bake in a preheated oven at 180°C/350°F/Gas Mark 4 for about 10-12 minutes, until the eggs are set and cooked. Serve sprinkled with chopped coriander and garnished with avocado slices.

PREPARATION: 25 MINUTES
COOKING: 10-12 MINUTES
SERVES: 4

AGUACATES RELLENOS

Stuffed avocados

2 tablespoons olive oil

1 teaspoon wine vinegar

juice of ½ lime

salt and freshly ground black pepper

2 avocados

For the stuffing:

3 tablespoons olive oil

1 onion, finely chopped

1 garlic clove, crushed

125g/4oz chopped mushrooms

1 red chilli, finely chopped

1 tablespoon chopped fresh coriander

To serve:

sour cream

warm tortillas

1 Make the dressing for the stuffed avocados: blend the olive oil with the wine vinegar and lime juice in a small bowl until thoroughly combined. Season with a little salt and some freshly ground black pepper.

2 Cut the avocados in half and remove the stones. Brush the inner surfaces of the avocado halves with the lime dressing; this will add flavour and prevent them browning. Set aside while you prepare the stuffing.

3 Heat the olive oil in a heavy frying pan and sauté the onion and garlic over low heat until soft and golden. Add the chopped mushrooms and chilli, and continue cooking for a few minutes, stirring occasionally, until cooked and golden brown. Stir in the coriander.

4 Remove from the heat and pile the stuffing mixture into the prepared avocados. Place on a lightly oiled baking tray and warm through in a preheated oven at 170°C/325°F/Gas Mark 3 for 10–15 minutes. Serve topped with sour cream, with warm tortillas.

PREPARATION: 25 MINUTES
COOKING: 10–15 MINUTES
SERVES: 4

GAZPACHO
Iced tomato soup

1 garlic clove

1 litre/1³/₄ pints tomato juice

3 tablespoons olive oil

2 tablespoons lemon juice

1 tablespoon lime juice

2 teaspoons sugar

salt and black pepper

150g/5oz diced peeled cucumber

75g/3oz chopped mild red onion or
spring onions

150g/5oz diced red pepper

75g/3oz diced avocado

2 tablespoons chopped mixed fresh herbs

For serving:

ice cubes

coarsely crushed tortilla chips

lime wedges

2 Pour the tomato juice into the bowl, and then add the olive oil, lemon and lime juices, sugar and salt and black pepper to taste.

3 Lightly beat the tomato juice with the other ingredients until well amalgamated. Cover the bowl with some cling film and chill in the refrigerator for at least 1 hour.

4 Beat the soup again and stir in the remaining ingredients. Place some ice cubes in individual serving bowls and pour the soup over the top. Sprinkle with coarsely crushed tortilla chips and serve with lime wedges.

1 Cut the garlic clove in half and then rub the cut surfaces over the bottom and around the sides of a large mixing bowl. Discard the garlic.

PREPARATION: 20 MINUTES
CHILLING: 1 HOUR
SERVES: 6–8

SOPA DE AGUACATE FRIA

Cold avocado soup

50g/2oz butter
4 tablespoons olive oil
1 onion, finely chopped
1 leek, finely chopped
1 carrot, finely chopped
2 garlic cloves, crushed
4 ripe avocados, peeled and stoned
250ml/8 fl oz natural yogurt
salt and ground black pepper
2 tablespoons lime juice
125ml/4 fl oz crème fraîche
2 tablespoons chopped fresh coriander

For the stock:

2 litres/3½ pints water
1 chicken carcass
1 onion, sliced
4 garlic cloves, halved
2 carrots
2 bay leaves
few black peppercorns
½ teaspoon salt
2 sticks celery

2 Melt the butter and oil in a large saucepan and sauté the onion, leek, carrot and garlic until tender. Add about 750ml/1¼ pints of the reserved chicken stock and simmer gently for about 30 minutes.

3 Process the avocados in batches with 1 litre/1¾ pints of the reserved stock in a food processor or blender until smooth. Add the vegetable mixture and continue to blend to a smooth green purée.

4 Stir in the yogurt and season to taste with salt and pepper. Add the lime juice, and thin with stock if necessary. Chill for 1 hour. Serve with a swirl of crème fraîche, sprinkled with chopped coriander.

1 Make the stock: bring the water to the boil in a large saucepan or stock pot and add the chicken, vegetables, herbs, spices and seasoning. Skim off any scum, lower the heat and simmer for 1½ hours. Cool and strain.

PREPARATION: 15 MINUTES
COOKING: 2 HOURS +
CHILLING TIME
SERVES: 6–8

SOPA DE FRIJOLES NEGROS
Black bean soup

1 Place the black beans in a bowl and cover with cold water. Leave them to soak overnight. The following day, drain the beans and rinse them well.

2 Put the beans in a large saucepan, cover with fresh, cold water and bring to the boil. Boil briskly for 10 minutes, drain and rinse well. Return the beans to the pan with the ham, onion, celery, garlic and measured water. Bring to the boil, skimming off any scum. Add the spices and herbs, cover and simmer for 3-4 hours.

PREPARATION: 6-8 HOURS
COOKING: 5¼ HOURS
SERVES: 4-6

3 Remove the ham (use in another dish) and discard the bay leaf. Let the bean mixture cool and then process in batches in a food processor or blender, reserving a few whole beans for decoration.

500g/1lb dried black beans
500-750g/1-1½ lb smoked ham hocks
1 large onion, quartered
1 celery stick, chopped
3 garlic cloves, peeled
2 litres/3½ pints water
1 teaspoon black peppercorns
4 whole cloves
½ teaspoon cumin seeds
1 bay leaf
2 teaspoons crushed garlic
salt
250ml/8 fl oz dry sherry
To garnish:
lemon slices

4 Sieve the puréed mixture into a clean saucepan and add the crushed garlic, and season to taste with salt. Simmer for 45 minutes and then stir in the sherry. Simmer for 20 minutes, until thick. Stir in the reserved beans and serve hot, garnished with lemon slices.

ALBONDIGAS DE CAMARONES

Mexican prawn soup

250g/8oz cooked prawns, shelled and finely chopped
2 tablespoons grated onion
1 tablespoon tomato paste
1 teaspoon ground cinnamon
1 teaspoon ground cumin
1 teaspoon chopped oregano
1 teaspoon ground coriander seeds
2 heaped tablespoons flour
1 egg yolk
pinch of salt

For the soup:

3 tablespoons olive oil
1 onion, thinly sliced
2 cloves garlic, crushed
500g/1lb beefsteak tomatoes, skinned and chopped
4 green chillies, seeded and chopped
1.5 litres/2½ pints fish stock
2 bay leaves
salt and freshly ground black pepper
2 tablespoons chopped fresh coriander

2 Make the soup: heat the olive oil in a large saucepan and sauté the sliced onion and garlic for 10 minutes, until soft. Add the chopped tomatoes and chillies and cook over low heat for 15 minutes.

3 Add the fish stock, bay leaves, salt and pepper, and then bring to the boil. Simmer the soup very gently for 30 minutes over low heat.

4 Divide the prawn mixture into 12 portions and shape into small balls. Drop them carefully into the soup. Poach very gently over low heat for 5 minutes. Remove the bay leaves and serve hot, sprinkled with chopped coriander.

1 Put the chopped prawns in a bowl with the onion, tomato paste, spices, herbs, flour, egg yolk and salt. Mix well until thoroughly blended, then cover the bowl and chill in the refrigerator for 30 minutes.

PREPARATION: 20 MINUTES
COOKING: 1 HOUR
SERVES: 4–6

SOPA DE TORTILLA
Tortilla soup

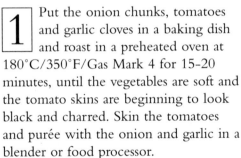

1 Put the onion chunks, tomatoes and garlic cloves in a baking dish and roast in a preheated oven at 180°C/350°F/Gas Mark 4 for 15–20 minutes, until the vegetables are soft and the tomato skins are beginning to look black and charred. Skin the tomatoes and purée with the onion and garlic in a blender or food processor.

1 large onion, cut in chunks
3 large tomatoes
3 garlic cloves, peeled
4 tablespoons olive oil
1 litre/1¾ pints chicken stock
salt and freshly ground black pepper
6 x 1-day-old tortillas
oil for shallow frying
2 fresh red or green chillies, seeded and chopped

To serve:

chopped avocado
sour cream
lime wedges

2 Heat 2 tablespoons of the oil and sauté the puréed mixture for a few minutes. Simmer until it is thick and reduced. Add the chicken stock and bring to the boil. Reduce the heat, season with salt and pepper and simmer, covered, for 15–20 minutes.

3 Cut the tortillas into thin strips and shallow fry in some oil until golden brown. Drain on some absorbent kitchen paper and then add to the soup. Simmer gently for a further 5 minutes.

4 Fry the chillies in the remaining olive oil in a small frying pan until crisp. Serve the soup garnished with the fried chilli, some chopped avocado, sour cream and lime wedges.

PREPARATION: 20–25 MINUTES
COOKING: 35–40 MINUTES
SERVES: 4–6

SEVICHE

Marinated fish

500g/1lb mixed fish, e.g fillets of sole, flounder, haddock, scallops and prawns
125ml/4 fl oz lime juice
2 tomatoes
½ teaspoon dried red chilli pepper flakes
1 tablespoon olive oil
½ teaspoon salt
pinch of dried oregano
freshly ground black pepper
For the garnish:
peeled, sliced avocado
2 tablespoons chopped fresh coriander
2 limes, cut into wedges

1 Clean and rinse the fish in cold water, and pat dry with absorbent kitchen paper. Cut the fish and scallops (if using) into thin slices. Shell and devein the prawns.

2 Place all the fish in a ceramic bowl and pour the lime juice over the top. Cover and then refrigerate for about 3-4 hours.

3 Put the tomatoes in a bowl and cover with boiling water. Leave for 1 minute and then plunge them into a bowl of cold water and skin them. Chop them roughly.

4 Stir in the chilli pepper flakes, tomato, olive oil, salt, oregano and pepper. Mix well and refrigerate for 2-3 hours. Stand at room temperature for 15 minutes before serving, garnished with avocado, chopped coriander and lime wedges.

PREPARATION: 15 MINUTES
MARINATING: 3-4 HOURS
SERVES: 4

HUACHINANGO EN CILANTRO

Red snapper in coriander

1kg/2lb red snapper or other white fish fillets

4 tablespoons lime or lemon juice

2 teaspoons salt

4 tablespoons olive oil

25g/1oz fresh breadcrumbs

1 garlic clove, crushed

6 tablespoons crushed coriander leaves

1 teaspoon grated lime or lemon rind

freshly ground black pepper

For serving:

warmed tortillas

2 Add sufficient cold water to cover the fish and then simmer gently over low heat for 5 minutes, turning twice during the cooking time.

3 In another pan, heat half of the olive oil, and add the breadcrumbs, garlic, remaining salt and 4 tablespoons of the coriander. Cook over a low heat, stirring constantly, until the crumbs are golden brown. Spread over the fish and simmer for 7-10 minutes, until the fish flakes easily.

1 Rinse the fish fillets under running cold water and pat dry with absorbent kitchen paper. Rub the fish with half of the lime or lemon juice and 1 teaspoon of the salt, and place, skin side down, in a lightly oiled heavy frying pan.

4 Blend the remaining lime or lemon juice and oil together, and pour over the fish. Cook for 2-3 minutes. Combine the remaining coriander with the grated lime or lemon rind and sprinkle over the fish. Season with black pepper and serve hot with warmed tortillas.

PREPARATION: 10 MINUTES
COOKING: 20 MINUTES
SERVES: 4

PESCADO VERACRUZ

Veracruz-style fish

4 tablespoons olive oil

2 onions, chopped

1 garlic clove, crushed

2 fresh hot red chillies, seeded and finely chopped

4 large tomatoes, skinned and chopped

8 stuffed green olives, chopped

4 stoned black olives, chopped

1 tablespoon chopped capers

pinch of dried oregano

1kg/2lb sea bass or red snapper fillets

40g/1½oz plain flour

salt

50g/2oz butter

2 tablespoons chopped fresh coriander

1 Heat the oil in a frying pan, add the onion and garlic and fry gently until soft and golden. Stir in the chilli, chopped tomatoes, olives, capers and oregano. Bring to the boil, reduce the heat and simmer the mixture gently for 20 minutes.

3 Melt the butter in a large frying pan, add the fish fillets and fry gently for about 5 minutes on each side until cooked and golden.

2 Wash the sea bass or red snapper fillets and pat dry on absorbent kitchen paper. Mix the flour with a little salt to season it in a dish, and then use to coat the fish fillets, shaking off any excess flour.

4 Transfer the fish fillets to a heated serving dish and pour the tomato sauce over the top. Sprinkle with chopped coriander and serve with warm tortillas, salad and rice.

PREPARATION: 15 MINUTES
COOKING: 35 MINUTES
SERVES: 4-6

PESCADO MEXICANO

Mexican fish stew

3 tablespoons olive oil

1 large onion, chopped

2 garlic cloves, crushed

1 large red pepper, seeded and chopped

1 large yellow pepper, seeded and chopped

500g/1lb tomatoes, skinned and chopped

2 tablespoons finely chopped fresh ginger

1 tablespoon chopped fresh coriander

2 teaspoons chopped fresh oregano

grated rind of 1 lime

few drops of hot chilli sauce

2-4 dried red chillies, chopped

1.2kg/2½lb monkfish

300ml/½ pint fish stock

12 scallops, halved

250g/8oz uncooked prawns

salt and freshly ground black pepper

torn coriander leaves

2 Add the tomato, ginger, chopped coriander, oregano, lime rind, chilli sauce and dried red chillies. Stir well to mix thoroughly and then simmer the mixture gently over low heat for 10 minutes.

3 Cut the monkfish into chunks, removing any bone and skin. Add the monkfish and fish stock to the saucepan and bring to the boil. Reduce the heat and then simmer gently for 20 minutes.

1 Heat the oil in a large heavy-based saucepan and gently sauté the onion, garlic and the red and yellow peppers for about 10-15 minutes, until they are tender.

4 Stir in the scallops and prawns and cook gently for 2 more minutes, until cooked. Season to taste with salt and pepper and serve the fish stew with warm tortillas garnished with torn coriander leaves.

PREPARATION: 15 MINUTES
COOKING: 45 MINUTES
SERVES: 6

ENCHILADAS DE JAIBA

Crab-stuffed tortillas

oil for shallow frying

12 soft corn tortillas

450ml/³/₄ pint red chilli sauce (see page 110)

500g/1lb crabmeat

250g/8oz grated Cheddar cheese

125g/4oz diced Mozzarella cheese

1 small red onion, finely chopped

3 tablespoons chopped fresh coriander

For the garnish:

sour cream and guacamole

3 Put some crabmeat on the middle of each tortilla. Sprinkle some grated Cheddar cheese and diced Mozzarella on top (reserving a little) and then add some chopped red onion. Roll up the tortillas and place them in a well-buttered ovenproof dish.

1 Heat the oil in a large shallow frying pan and shallow-fry the tortillas, one at a time, over moderate heat for a few seconds until they become limp. Take care not to overcook the tortillas – they must not be allowed to become crisp.

2 Pat the tortillas with absorbent kitchen paper and then spread each one with a little of the prepared red chilli sauce.

4 Pour the remaining red chilli sauce over the top of the tortillas and scatter with the rest of the cheese. Bake in a preheated oven at 200°C/400°F/Gas Mark 6 for 15–20 minutes. Garnish with chopped coriander, and serve the enchiladas with sour cream and guacamole.

PREPARATION: 15 MINUTES
COOKING: 15-20 MINUTES
SERVES: 4-6

EMPANADAS DE CAMARONES

Prawn turnovers

1 Heat the oil in a frying pan, add the onion and garlic and sauté over low heat until soft and golden. Stir in the tomato paste, prawns, chilli, cumin, allspice, oregano, lemon juice and seasoning. Cook gently until the mixture reduces and thickens a little, then set aside to cool.

2 tablespoons olive oil
1 large onion, finely chopped
2 garlic cloves, crushed
4 tablespoons tomato paste
500g/1lb cooked prawns, chopped
4 green chillies, seeded and finely chopped
1 teaspoon ground cumin
1 teaspoon ground allspice
2 teaspoons oregano
1 tablespoon lemon juice
salt and freshly ground pepper to taste
1 quantity tortilla dough (see page 10)
oil for deep frying

To serve:

salsa and guacamole

2 Roll out the tortilla dough and make about 20 tortillas, 7.5cm/3 inches in diameter. Place a small spoonful of the cooled prawn mixture in the centre of each tortilla.

PREPARATION: 25 MINUTES
COOKING: 20-25 MINUTES
SERVES: 5-6

3 Fold the dough over the prawn filling and dampen and press the edges together firmly between your fingers to seal them. Repeat in this way until all the empanadas are sealed. If wished, cover with cling film and chill in the refrigerator until you are ready to cook and serve them.

4 Heat the oil in a large saucepan and deep fry the empanadas until they are golden all over. Drain on absorbent kitchen paper and serve hot with salsa and guacamole.

CAMARONES ACAPULQUENOS
Acapulco-style prawns

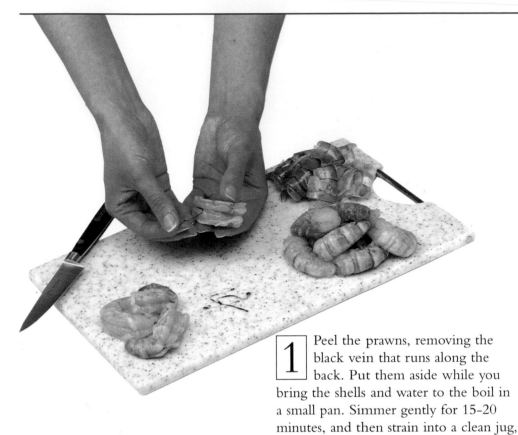

3. Add the tomatoes, tomato paste and lime juice. Season to taste with salt and freshly ground black pepper, and simmer for 10-15 minutes until the mixture thickens and reduces.

1. Peel the prawns, removing the black vein that runs along the back. Put them aside while you bring the shells and water to the boil in a small pan. Simmer gently for 15-20 minutes, and then strain into a clean jug, discarding the shells.

500g/1lb uncooked large prawns
300ml/½ pint water
25g/1oz butter
½ onion, finely chopped
3 garlic cloves, crushed
1 green chilli, finely chopped
3 tablespoons chopped fresh parsley
3 large tomatoes, skinned and chopped
2 tablespoons tomato paste
juice of 1 lime
salt and freshly ground black pepper
To garnish:
2 tablespoons chopped fresh parsley
wedges of lime
boiled rice

PREPARATION: 30 MINUTES
COOKING: 20-25 MINUTES
SERVES: 4

4. Add the reserved prawn liquid and simmer for 5 minutes, stirring occasionally. Gently stir in the peeled prawns and cook for a further 2-3 minutes until they turn pink. Serve garnished with chopped parsley and lime wedges on a bed of rice.

2. Heat the butter in a large heavy-based frying pan and sauté the onion and garlic until soft and golden. Add the chilli and parsley, and sauté, stirring, for about 2 minutes, until the parsley turns dark green.

CAMARONES AL CARBON
Seafood brochettes

1 Prepare the seafood: peel the prawns and remove the black vein running along the back. Remove any bones from the tuna and cut into large chunks. Wash the scallops and pat them dry. If they are very large, cut them in half.

2 Make the marinade: put the squeezed juice of 2 limes with the olive oil and garlic in a large bowl. Mix thoroughly to blend and add some salt and pepper. Put the prepared seafood in the marinade and stir gently until it is completely coated. Cover and refrigerate for at least 1 hour.

3 Remove the seafood from the marinade and thread alternately on to wooden or metal skewers. Place them on the rack of a grill pan and brush with the remaining marinade. Grill, turning occasionally, until cooked and tender – this takes about 5 minutes. Baste with more marinade if necessary.

500g/1lb mixed seafood (e.g. uncooked prawns, fresh tuna, scallops)
juice of 2 limes
2 tablespoons olive oil
2 garlic cloves, crushed
salt and freshly ground black pepper
50g/2oz softened butter
2 hot chillies (preferably jalapeño)
few coriander leaves, torn
To serve:
plain boiled rice

4 Make the chilli butter: blend the softened butter with the chopped chillies until they are thoroughly mixed. Arrange the seafood brochettes on 4 serving plates on a bed of rice and put a pat of chilli butter on top of each one. Scatter with torn coriander leaves.

PREPARATION: 20 MINUTES +
1 HOUR MARINATING
COOKING: 5 MINUTES
SERVES: 4

CAMARONES AL MOJO DE AJO
Garlic prawns

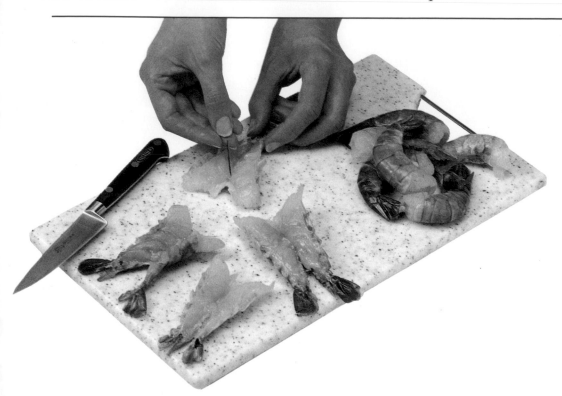

3 Coat the prepared prawns with this garlic mixture and place them in a bowl. Scrape out any of the remaining garlic paste over the top, then cover the bowl and leave in a cool place to marinate for at least 1 hour.

1 Prepare the prawns: remove the heads and, leaving them in their shells, split them carefully down the middle towards the tail end without completely separating them. They should look a little like butterflies. Remove the dark vein running along the back of the prawns.

24 uncooked king-size prawns
6 garlic cloves
sea salt and whole black peppercorns
2 red chillies, seeded and chopped
3 tablespoons olive oil
50g/2oz butter
juice of 2 limes
3 tablespoons chopped fresh coriander

To serve:

lime wedges
sliced avocado
warm tortillas

PREPARATION: 15 MINUTES +
1 HOUR MARINATING
COOKING: 5 MINUTES
SERVES: 4-6

2 Peel the garlic cloves and then crush them with the sea salt, peppercorns and the chopped chillies in a pestle and mortar, until you have a thick aromatic paste.

4 Heat the olive oil and butter in a large heavy-based frying pan and add the prawns and the garlic paste. Quickly sauté them over medium heat for 2-3 minutes, until they turn pink. Remove from the pan and keep warm. Add the lime juice to the pan and stir into the pan juices. Boil vigorously for a couple of minutes and then pour over the prawns. Serve sprinkled with coriander, with lime wedges, sliced avocado and freshly-made warm tortillas.

MOLE DE POLLO

Chicken stew

4 chicken portions
1 garlic clove, crushed
1 onion, chopped
1 dried red chilli pepper, seeded and chopped
475ml/16 fl oz water or chicken stock
1 fresh green or red chilli, chopped
75g/3oz flaked almonds
75g/3oz fresh breadcrumbs
1/2 teaspoon ground cinnamon
1/2 teaspoon ground cloves
1 tablespoon sesame seeds
25g/1oz lard
400g/14oz canned tomatoes, drained and chopped
25g/1oz plain dark chocolate, grated
salt and pepper
2 tablespoons sesame seeds, toasted
2 limes, cut into wedges
few fresh coriander leaves

2 In a blender or food processor, blend together the chilli, almonds, breadcrumbs, cinnamon, cloves and sesame seeds. Add about half of the reserved chicken stock and blend until smooth.

4 Add the chicken pieces and bring to the boil. Cook gently to heat the chicken through, and then transfer to a serving dish. Serve sprinkled with toasted sesame seeds garnished with lime wedges and coriander leaves.

3 Heat the lard in a heavy frying pan and stir in the breadcrumb mixture. Fry gently for 2 minutes and then add the tomatoes. Gradually stir in the remaining stock, together with the grated chocolate. Simmer gently for 5 minutes and season to taste.

1 Simmer the chicken portions with the garlic, onion and dried chilli pepper in the water or chicken stock for 40 minutes, or until the chicken is tender. Cool slightly, strain the stock and skim off any fat. Measure out 450ml/3/4 pint and set aside. Remove the skin and bones from the chicken and cut into neat pieces.

PREPARATION: 20 MINUTES
COOKING: 1 HOUR
SERVES: 4

FAJITAS DE POLLO

Chicken-stuffed tortillas

6 chicken breast fillets, skinned and boned and cut into strips

2 large onions, peeled and sliced

1 red pepper, seeded and cut into strips

1 green pepper, seeded and cut into strips

2 tablespoons olive oil

12 soft tortillas, warmed

250g/8oz guacamole

300ml/½ pint sour cream

2 tablespoons toasted sesame seeds

1 tablespoon chopped fresh coriander

For the marinade:

juice of 4 limes

3 tablespoons olive oil

1 teaspoon dried oregano

1 teaspoon dried coriander

2 Put the chicken strips and marinade in a roasting pan. Cover with foil and bake in a preheated oven at 200°C/400°F/Gas Mark 6 for 30 minutes. Bake uncovered for the last 10 minutes of the cooking time. Slice the chicken into thin strips.

1 Make the marinade: combine the lime juice with the oil, dried oregano and coriander in a bowl. Add the chicken strips and stir well. Cover and leave in the refrigerator for 4 hours.

PREPARATION: 15 MINUTES
MARINATING: 4 HOURS
COOKING: 45 MINUTES
SERVES: 4

3 Meanwhile, sauté the onions and peppers in the oil until they are soft and melting. It does not matter if they become a little brown and caramelized.

4 Place a little of the sautéed onions and peppers on each warmed tortilla and top with some chicken. Add a little guacamole, some sour cream and sesame seeds. Sprinkle with coriander and roll up. Serve with salsa if wished.

POLLO CON NARANJAS

Orange chicken

1 teaspoon salt

¼ teaspoon ground cinnamon

⅛ teaspoon ground cloves

4 chicken portions

2 tablespoons oil

1 onion, chopped

2 garlic cloves, crushed

150ml/¼ pint fresh orange juice

150ml/¼ pint chicken stock

2 tablespoons raisins

2 green chillies, seeded and sliced

50g/2oz slivered almonds

3 oranges, peeled and thinly sliced

2 tablespoons chopped fresh coriander

2 Heat the oil in a large frying pan, add the chicken and fry, turning occasionally, until all the chicken pieces are browned all over. Remove them from the pan and pour off any excess fat. Keep the chicken warm.

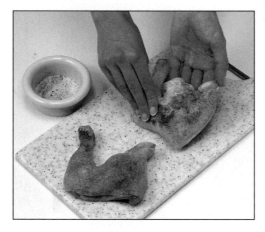

1 Mix the salt, ground cinnamon and cloves together, and then rub this spicy mixture all over the chicken portions to flavour them.

3 Add the onion and garlic to the pan, and sauté gently until tender and golden. Return the chicken to the pan and stir in the orange juice, chicken stock, raisins and chillies. Cover the pan and simmer for 1 hour, or until the chicken is cooked and tender.

4 Add the almonds and the orange slices, and stir gently. Heat through over low heat for about 5 minutes. Serve the orange chicken sprinkled with chopped coriander.

PREPARATION: 15 MINUTES
COOKING: 1½ HOURS
SERVES: 4

POLLO AL CARBON

Marinated chicken kebabs

juice of 2 limes or lemons

1 tablespoon honey

1 green chilli, finely chopped

2 tablespoons olive oil

6 chicken breasts

For the avocado sauce:

3 tablespoons olive oil

1 tablespoon red wine vinegar

1 large avocado, peeled, stoned and mashed

1 large tomato, skinned and chopped

2 spring onions, chopped

120ml/4 fl oz sour cream

seeds of 1 pomegranate

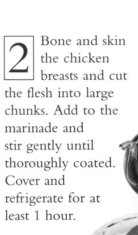

2 Bone and skin the chicken breasts and cut the flesh into large chunks. Add to the marinade and stir gently until thoroughly coated. Cover and refrigerate for at least 1 hour.

1 Make the marinade: squeeze the lime or lemon juice into a large bowl and mix in the honey, chopped chilli and olive oil, until the mixture is well blended and smooth.

PREPARATION: 15 MINUTES +
1 HOUR MARINATING
COOKING: 15 MINUTES
SERVES: 4

3 Thread the chicken on to wooden skewers and brush with the marinade. Place under a preheated hot grill or cook on a barbecue, turning occasionally, until the chicken is cooked, tender and golden brown. Brush the kebabs with more marinade if necessary.

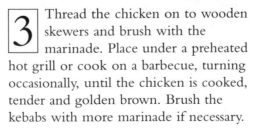

4 Meanwhile, make the avocado sauce: blend the olive oil and vinegar together in a bowl and then beat in the mashed avocado until thick and smooth. Stir in the chopped tomato and spring onions, and then the sour cream. Serve the kebabs accompanied by a mound of avocado sauce, scattered with pomegranate seeds.

POSOLE

Pork and chicken stew

1 Put the cubed pork, ribs and onion in a large saucepan and pour in 2 litres/3½ pints of the water. Bring to the boil, skimming off any scum. Add the garlic, lower the heat and then simmer for 1 hour. Add the chicken and the remaining water and simmer for 30 minutes.

350g/12oz boneless pork shoulder, cubed
250g/8oz pork ribs
1 large onion, quartered
3 litres/5½ pints water
2 garlic cloves, crushed
1-1.25kg/2-2½lb chicken, cut in serving pieces
1 tablespoon vegetable oil
175g/6oz chopped onion
4 tablespoons chilli powder
salt and black pepper
175g/6oz canned hominy or corn kernels

For serving:

shredded lettuce or cabbage
sliced radishes
chopped spring onions
chopped tomato
lime wedges

PREPARATION: 15 MINUTES
COOKING: 2 HOURS
SERVES: 4-6

2 Remove the chicken, ribs and pork. Discard the onion and strain the stock into a bowl. Dice the chicken, ribs and pork cubes, discarding any skin and bones.

3 Heat the oil and sauté the chopped onion until soft and golden. Stir in the chilli powder, the reserved stock and salt and pepper to taste. Bring to the boil, then reduce the heat and add the hominy or corn kernels. Simmer gently for 15 minutes.

4 Add all the diced meat and simmer for a further 10 minutes. Serve piping hot topped with shredded lettuce or cabbage and sliced radishes, with spring onions, chopped tomato and lime wedges.

PICADILLO

Beef stew

75g/3oz lard or bacon fat

675g/1½ lb minced beef

1 large onion, finely chopped

4 tablespoons red wine

3 tablespoons lime juice

2 tomatoes, skinned and chopped

2 small hot green chillies, chopped

75g/3oz stuffed green olives, sliced

2 cooking apples, peeled, cored
and chopped

3 tablespoons capers

75g/3oz raisins

2 large potatoes, peeled
and cut into small cubes

1 garlic clove, crushed

½ teaspoon ground cumin

salt

50g/2oz chopped blanched almonds, toasted

2 Reduce the heat and add the wine and lime juice. Cook for 5 minutes and stir in the tomatoes, chillies, olives, apple, capers and raisins. Cover and simmer for 20 minutes.

3 Heat the remaining fat in another pan. Fry the potatoes, garlic and cumin, turning occasionally, until evenly golden brown. Lower the heat and cook for 10-12 minutes until the potatoes are tender.

4 Add the potatoes to the meat mixture and cook gently for 5 minutes. Season to taste, transfer to a warm serving dish and sprinkle with the toasted almonds.

1 Heat half of the lard or bacon fat in a heavy frying pan. Add the beef and onion and cook over high heat, stirring constantly, until evenly browned.

PREPARATION: 15 MINUTES
COOKING: 35 MINUTES
SERVES: 4

TACOS
Fried stuffed tortillas

500g/1lb minced steak

75g/3oz chopped onion

65g/2½oz chopped green pepper

1 garlic clove, crushed

1 teaspoon dried oregano

½ teaspoon hot paprika

¼ teaspoon ground cumin

¼ teaspoon dried hot red chilli pepper flakes

salt and black pepper

125ml/4 fl oz tomato paste

12 tortillas

oil for frying

For serving:

shredded lettuce

finely chopped tomatoes

grated Cheddar cheese

diced avocado

sour cream

salsa cruda (see page 111)

2 Add the onion, green pepper and garlic and cook, stirring occasionally, until softened. Stir in the herbs, spices and seasoning to taste.

3 Add the tomato paste and mix well. Cover and cook gently for 10 minutes, stirring occasionally.

1 Cook the minced steak in a frying pan until brown and crumbly, stirring occasionally and breaking it up with a wooden spoon.

4 Place a little of the mixture on each tortilla and roll up. Secure with a cocktail stick and then fry quickly in a little oil until golden. Serve with the various accompaniments.

PREPARATION: 15 MINUTES
COOKING: 30 MINUTES
SERVES: 4–6

CHILE VERDE

Green chilli stew

1 Heat 3 tablespoons of the olive oil in a large heavy-based casserole and cook the stewing steak in batches, turning occasionally, over medium heat until lightly browned. Remove from the pan with a slotted spoon and keep warm. Pour off the meat juices and reserve.

2 Cut the green peppers into 2.5cm/1 inch squares. Heat the remaining oil in the casserole and sauté the green pepper and garlic over low heat for 5 minutes until the pepper is cooked and tender.

PREPARATION: 10 MINUTES
COOKING: 2½ HOURS
SERVES: 4

3 Return the meat to the pan, and add the chilli, chopped tomatoes, brown sugar, cloves, cinnamon, cumin, lime juice and beef stock or wine. Bring to the boil, stirring continuously. Cover the casserole and cook in a preheated oven at 190°C/375°F/Gas Mark 5 for 1¾ hours.

5 tablespoons olive oil
1kg/2lb stewing steak, cubed
3 green peppers
3 garlic cloves, crushed
4 fresh green chillies, seeded and finely sliced
475g/15oz canned chopped tomatoes
2 teaspoons brown sugar
¼ teaspoon ground cloves
¼ teaspoon ground cinnamon
2 teaspoons ground cumin
4 tablespoons lime juice
325ml/11 fl oz beef stock or red wine
salt and freshly ground black pepper
3 tablespoons chopped coriander

4 Remove the casserole from the oven, uncover and simmer gently on top of the stove for 20 minutes, or until the sauce has reduced and thickened. Season to taste with salt and freshly ground black pepper. Serve garnished with chopped coriander.

TOSTADAS

Fried beef tortillas

8 tortillas

oil for frying

500g/1lb minced beef

2 red chillies, chopped

2 garlic cloves, crushed

½ teaspoon ground cumin

125ml/4 fl oz tomato paste

175ml/6 fl oz beef stock

1 tablespoon vinegar

2 tomatoes, skinned and chopped

For serving:

shredded lettuce

grated cheese

stoned black olives

2 Put the minced beef in a clean frying pan and fry it gently in its own fat until it is cooked and browned, breaking it up as it cooks. Pour off and discard any excess fat.

3 Add the chopped chilli, garlic, cumin, tomato paste, beef stock and vinegar. Bring to the boil, stirring, and add the tomatoes. Reduce the heat and cook gently for 10-15 minutes until reduced and thickened.

4 Place a large spoonful of the meat mixture on each tostada(fried tortilla). Top with the shredded lettuce, grated cheese and the olives.

1 Fry the tortillas in about 5mm/¼ inch oil in a large frying pan until they are crisp and golden – about 1 minute on each side. Keep warm while you make the topping.

PREPARATION: 20 MINUTES
COOKING: 25-30 MINUTES
SERVES: 4

CHORIZO ENCHILADAS

Meat-stuffed tortillas in chilli sauce

500g/1lb minced pork
500g/1lb minced beef
1 tablespoon olive oil
1 large onion, finely chopped
2 garlic cloves, crushed
1 tablespoon chilli powder
1/2 teaspoon ground cumin
2 teaspoons dried oregano
pinch of salt
50ml/2 fl oz vinegar
250ml/8 fl oz beef stock
450ml/3/4 pint red chilli sauce (see page 110)
oil for deep frying
12 corn or wheat tortillas
75g/3oz grated Cheddar or Monterey Jack cheese

To serve:

guacamole (see page 12)
sliced olives

2 Spread a little of the chilli sauce over the base of 1 large or 2 small shallow baking dishes. Heat the oil in a deep frying pan and fry the tortillas quickly on both sides – do not allow them to crisp up. Remove them with a slotted spoon and drain on absorbent kitchen paper.

3 Dip the tortillas into the chilli sauce and put about 2 tablespoons of the meat filling down the centre of each tortilla. Fold over and arrange in the baking dish(es).

4 Pour the remaining chilli sauce over the top and scatter with the grated cheese. Bake in a preheated oven at 180°C/350°F/Gas Mark 4 for 20-30 minutes until bubbling and golden brown. Serve with guacamole, garnished with olives.

1 Put the minced pork and beef in a frying pan and cook in their own fat until browned and crumbly, breaking up the meat with a spoon. Add the oil, onion and garlic and cook until soft. Stir in the chilli powder, cumin, oregano and salt, and then the vinegar and stock. Simmer for 10 minutes, or until the liquid has evaporated. Remove from the heat and cool.

PREPARATION: 40 MINUTES
COOKING: 20-30 MINUTES
SERVES: 6

EMPANADAS

Spicy pork pasties

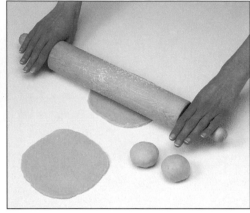

250g/8oz flour	
¼ teaspoon salt	
6 tablespoons lard, diced	
4 tablespoons butter, diced	
6–8 tablespoons iced water	
beaten egg for glaze	
sesame seeds	
For the filling:	
1½ tablespoons oil	
75g/3oz chopped onion	
1 garlic clove, crushed	
250g/8oz pork fillet, diced	
175g/6oz firmly packed shredded sweet potato	
4 juicy prunes, stoned	
125ml/4 fl oz unsweetened pineapple juice	
1 tablespoon tomato paste	
2 teaspoons chilli powder	
salt	

1 Make the filling: heat the oil in a frying pan and sauté the onion and garlic until soft. Add the pork and cook, stirring, until lightly browned. Stir in the remaining ingredients and continue cooking until the excess liquid has evaporated. Remove from the heat and cool.

3 Divide the dough into 8 equal portions and roll them out on a lightly floured surface to make 15cm/6 inch rounds.

2 Put the flour, salt and fats in a food processor, and process until the mixture resembles crumbs. Add enough iced water to make a soft dough. Shape into a ball and chill for 20–30 minutes.

PREPARATION: 30 MINUTES
+ CHILLING
COOKING: 35–40 MINUTES
SERVES: 4–6

4 Put one-eighth of the filling on each round. Dampen the edges and fold over to make half-moon shapes. Press the edges together and crimp with a fork. Place on a greased baking sheet, brush with beaten egg and sprinkle with sesame seeds. Bake in a preheated oven at 190°C/375°F/ Gas Mark 5 for 35–40 minutes.

BURRITOS DE PUERCO

Pork-stuffed tortillas

1kg/2lb boneless rolled pork shoulder

1 tablespoon oil

salt

350ml/12 fl oz meat stock

250ml/8 fl oz tomato paste

½ teaspoon grated orange rind

1 teaspoon dried hot red chilli flakes

8 medium-sized flour tortillas

To serve:

guacamole, sour cream and refried beans

2 While the pork is cooking, make the sauce. Put the meat stock in a small saucepan with the tomato paste, orange rind and dried chilli flakes. Bring to the boil, then reduce the heat and simmer gently for about 30 minutes until the sauce is reduced and thickened.

3 Remove any fat from the cooked pork and tear the meat into shreds, using a fork. Add to the sauce and heat through very gently over a low heat.

4 Wrap the flour tortillas in foil and heat through gently in a warm oven. Place a little of the pork mixture in the centre of each tortilla and then roll up. Serve with guacamole, sour cream and refried beans.

1 Put the pork shoulder in a roasting pan and brush with a little oil. Sprinkle with salt, and cook in a preheated oven at 180°C/ 350°F/Gas Mark 4 for about 1½ hours, or until crisp, golden and cooked through.

PREPARATION: 20 MINUTES
COOKING: 1½ HOURS
SERVES: 4

ARROZ VERDE

Green rice

1 Heat the lard in a heavy frying pan and stir in the rice. Cook, stirring frequently, until all the grains of rice are coated with fat and glistening.

2 Add the onion, garlic and tomatoes, and cook for 2 minutes. Add about 350ml/12 fl oz of the stock, cover the pan and simmer gently for about 25 minutes, or until the rice is tender and has absorbed all the liquid. Keep checking the rice and adding more stock as necessary. Season with salt and pepper.

PREPARATION: 10 MINUTES
COOKING: 30 MINUTES
SERVES: 4

3 Five minutes before the end of cooking time, heat the oil in another frying pan, and stir-fry the pepper strips until they start to lose their crispness. However, they should still retain their bright green colour.

4 Add the stir-fried pepper strips to the cooked rice, and stir in gently. Scatter with the sliced olives and serve immediately.

40g/1½oz lard
175g/6oz long-grain rice
1 onion, finely chopped
1 garlic clove, crushed
400g/14oz canned tomatoes, drained and chopped
450ml/¾ pint stock
salt and pepper
2 tablespoons vegetable oil
2 green peppers, seeded and cut into thin strips
125g/4oz pimiento-stuffed green olives, sliced

ARROZ A LA MEXICANA

Mexican rice

250g/8oz long-grain rice
4 tablespoons olive oil
2 garlic cloves, crushed
1 small onion, grated
1 red pepper, seeded and chopped
1 large tomato, skinned, seeded and chopped
1 tablespoon finely chopped fresh coriander
1 tablespoon ground cumin
600–750ml/1–1¼ pints chicken or beef stock
salt and freshly ground black pepper

1 Place the rice in a sieve and rinse thoroughly with cold running water to remove any excess starch. Drain and tip the rice into a large bowl, then cover with hot water. Leave to stand for 30 minutes.

2 Drain the rice thoroughly in a sieve, and then leave it in the sieve placed over a bowl for about 1 hour until it is really dry.

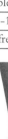

3 Heat the oil in a heavy frying pan and add the rice. Cook, stirring, over low heat until all the grains are well coated with oil, glistening and translucent. Add the garlic and onion and cook until they are transparent and the rice is golden.

4 Add the red pepper, tomato, coriander, cumin and stock. Stir well, cover the pan and cook gently over very low heat for 20–30 minutes, until all the liquid has been absorbed and the grains of rice are tender and fluffy. Season with salt and pepper to taste and serve hot as an accompaniment to a main dish.

PREPARATION: 1½ HOURS
COOKING: 30–40 MINUTES
SERVES: 4

ARROZ CON MARISCOS

Rice with seafood

1 Prepare the seafood: wash and clean the octopus or squid and cut into rings. Cut the tentacles into small pieces. Wash and peel the prawns. Cut the white fish into large chunks.

1kg/2lb mixed seafood, e.g. octopus, squid, prawns, white fish
2 tablespoons olive oil
1 large onion, chopped
2 garlic cloves, crushed
250g/8oz long-grain rice
600-750ml/1-1¼ pints fish stock
3 tomatoes, skinned and chopped
2 tablespoons chopped fresh parsley
salt and freshly ground black pepper
4 red or green chillies
To serve:
lime wedges and fresh coriander

2 Heat the oil in a large deep frying pan and sauté the onion and garlic until soft and golden. Add the rice and stir gently for a couple of minutes until all the grains are glistening with oil and slightly translucent.

PREPARATION: 15 MINUTES
COOKING: 45 MINUTES
SERVES: 4

3 Add some of the fish stock together with the chopped tomatoes and bring to the boil. Reduce the heat and simmer gently, adding more stock as and when necessary until all the liquid has been absorbed and the rice is tender. After 15 minutes, add the prepared seafood. Stir in the parsley and season to taste with salt and pepper when the rice is cooked.

4 Place a lightly oiled small frying pan over medium to high heat and, when it is hot, add the chillies. Press them down hard with a spatula against the surface of the pan for about 1 minute each side until they change colour. Take care that they do not burn. This helps to release their pungent aroma. Cut into thin strips and use as a garnish. Serve with lime wedges and coriander.

FRIJOLES REFRITOS

Refried beans

| 250g/8oz dried pinto beans |
| 4 garlic cloves, crushed |
| 1 bay leaf |
| 4 tablespoons lard or bacon fat |
| 180g/6oz chopped onion |
| salt and freshly ground black pepper |
| 50g/2oz grated Monterey Jack or Cheddar cheese |

1 Put the beans in a large bowl and cover with cold water. Leave to soak for at least 6 hours or, preferably, overnight. The following day, drain the beans and rinse them well under running cold water.

3 Drain the beans, reserving the cooking liquid. Discard the bay leaf. Mash the beans coarsely with a potato masher, or process in a blender or food processor, adding some of the reserved liquid as necessary until you achieve the desired consistency.

4 Melt the lard in a frying pan and sauté the onion, stirring, until soft. Add the beans and seasoning and mix well. Simmer until piping hot, continuing to mash and add more liquid as necessary. Serve hot, sprinkled with cheese, with the garnish of your choice, e.g. guacamole, sour cream, sliced avocado or salsa.

2 Put the beans in a large saucepan with the garlic and bay leaf. Cover with cold water and bring to the boil. Boil briskly for 10 minutes, then lower the heat to a bare simmer and cook gently for about 2 hours, until the beans are very tender.

PREPARATION: 20 MINUTES +
6 HOURS SOAKING
COOKING: 2½ HOURS
SERVES: 4-6

FAJITAS DE CHILES

Vegetable fajitas

2 tablespoons olive oil

2 large onions, thinly sliced

2 garlic cloves, crushed

2 red peppers, thinly sliced

2 green peppers, thinly sliced

4 green chillies, seeded and thinly sliced

2 teaspoons chopped fresh oregano

250g/8oz button mushrooms, sliced

salt and freshly ground black pepper

To serve:

12 warmed tortillas

salsa and sour cream

2 Add the sliced red and green peppers, chillies and oregano and stir well. Sauté gently for 10 more minutes, until cooked and tender.

3 Add the sliced button mushrooms and cook quickly for 1 more minute, stirring to mix thoroughly with the other vegetables. Season the vegetable mixture with salt and black pepper to taste.

4 To serve, spoon the sizzling hot vegetable mixture into the warmed tortillas and fold over or roll up. Serve very hot with salsa and plenty of sour cream.

1 Heat the olive oil in a large frying pan and then gently sauté the sliced onions and garlic for about 5 minutes until they are soft and golden brown. They should be melting and almost caramelized.

PREPARATION: 15 MINUTES

COOKING: 16 MINUTES

SERVES: 4

GARBANZOS

Spicy chickpeas

300g/10oz dried chickpeas

1½ teaspoons salt

1 whole onion, peeled

6 rashers streaky bacon, chopped

2 onions, chopped

1 garlic clove, crushed

1 red pepper, seeded and chopped

¼ teaspoon ground black pepper

1 small dried hot red chilli, crumbled

½ teaspoon dried oregano

300g/10oz skinned and chopped tomatoes

2 tablespoons tomato paste

90ml/3½ fl oz water or reserved bean liquid

2 tablespoons chopped fresh coriander

2 Bring to the boil, and boil hard for 10 minutes. Reduce the heat and simmer, uncovered, for about 45 minutes, until the chickpeas are cooked and tender. Drain and reserve the cooking liquid.

3 Put the bacon in a frying pan and fry until the fat starts to run out of the bacon. Add the onions, garlic and red pepper and continue frying until soft. Stir in the remaining salt, the black pepper, chilli, oregano, tomatoes, tomato paste and some of the reserved bean liquid.

1 Soak the chickpeas overnight in cold water. Drain and place in a saucepan with 1 teaspoon of the salt and the whole peeled onion. Cover with cold water.

4 Add the drained chickpeas and stir well. Simmer for 10 minutes, stirring occasionally. Serve hot, sprinkled with chopped fresh coriander leaves.

PREPARATION: 1 HOUR +
SOAKING OVERNIGHT
COOKING: 30 MINUTES
SERVES: 4

VERDURAS CAPEADAS

Courgettes and cauliflower in batter

4 small courgettes

1 small head cauliflower, broken into florets

175g/6oz grated Cheddar or
Monterey Jack cheese

3 eggs, separated

salt and pepper

3 tablespoons flour

oil for deep frying

To serve:

1 quantity salsa de jitomate (see page 110)

1 Bring a large pan of boiling water to the boil and tip in all the courgettes and cauliflower florets. Boil rapidly for a few minutes, until the vegetables are just tender but still crisp. Remove from the heat and drain well.

2 Make a slit along the side of each courgette and scoop out a little of the flesh. Fill the hole with grated cheese. Stuff some of the grated cheese into the hollow of each cauliflower floret.

3 Beat the egg yolks lightly with the seasoning in a bowl. In another bowl, beat the egg whites until they are stiff and stand in peaks. Fold the beaten egg white gently into the yolks to make the batter.

4 Dip the cheese-filled vegetables in the flour and then into the batter. Heat the oil for deep frying and fry the vegetables in batches until crisp and golden. Remove with a slotted spoon. Drain on absorbent kitchen paper. Serve hot with salsa de jitomate.

PREPARATION: 20 MINUTES
COOKING: 5-10 MINUTES
SERVES: 4

ENSALADA DE NOCHE BUENA
Christmas Eve salad

1 Prepare all the fruits and sprinkle with lemon or lime juice to prevent any discolouration.

2 Make the dressing: mix all the ingredients together and blend thoroughly, or put in a screwtop jar and shake vigorously until the sugar has completely dissolved.

PREPARATION: 25 MINUTES
SERVES: 4-6

3 Line a large bowl with lettuce leaves and arrange the sliced beetroot and fruit on top in attractive concentric circles, finishing with the banana. Sprinkle the dressing over the top of the salad.

1 green apple, peeled, cored and sliced
2 oranges, peeled and sliced
½ fresh pineapple, peeled, cored and sliced
1 large banana, sliced
1 large red apple, cored and sliced
125ml/4 fl oz lemon or lime juice
1 large lettuce
2 small cooked beetroots, peeled and sliced
75g/3oz unsalted roasted peanuts
seeds of ½ small pomegranate
For the dressing:
6 tablespoons olive oil
2 tablespoons lemon or lime juice
1 teaspoon sugar
¼ teaspoon salt

4 Decorate the salad with the peanuts and pomegranate seeds and serve immediately.

FLAN

Mexican caramel custard

1 Put half of the sugar in a saucepan with a little water. Heat gently, stirring to dissolve the sugar. Boil briskly until the caramel turns golden. Pour a little into 6 dariole moulds or custard cups, rotating the moulds to cover them evenly.

3 Beat the egg and egg yolks together until light and frothy and then stir in the cooled milk.

2 Heat the milk in a heavy pan over low heat. Add the remaining sugar, salt, vanilla pod and cinnamon stick. Cook, stirring, for 2-3 minutes. Cool and remove the cinnamon stick and vanilla pod.

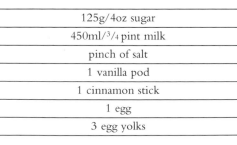

4 Strain the custard into the prepared moulds. Stand in a roasting pan containing about 2.5cm/1 inch hot water and cook in a preheated oven at 180°C/350°F/Gas Mark 4 for about 45 minutes, until set. Cool and chill. Unmould and serve decorated with cream and almonds.

125g/4oz sugar
450ml/³/₄ pint milk
pinch of salt
1 vanilla pod
1 cinnamon stick
1 egg
3 egg yolks
For decoration:
75ml/3 fl oz whipped cream
blanched almonds, toasted and crushed

PREPARATION: 20 MINUTES
COOKING: 45 MINUTES
SERVES 6

BUNUELOS

Mexican puffed fritters

250g/8oz plain flour
1 teaspoon baking powder
pinch of salt
1 tablespoon sugar
1 egg, well beaten
2 tablespoons melted lard
125ml/4 fl oz milk
oil for deep frying

For the syrup:

350ml/12 fl oz water
4 tablespoons sherry
125g/4oz dark brown sugar
½ cinnamon stick

1 Sift the flour, baking powder and salt into a large mixing bowl. Stir in the sugar and mix in the beaten egg, fat and enough milk to form a soft, but not too sticky, dough.

2 Divide the dough into 8–12 equal-sized pieces. With floured hands, shape each one into a ball. Cover with a sheet of plastic cling film and leave to stand for 30 minutes. Shape into flat cakes and make a shallow depression in the centre of each one.

3 Heat the oil to 190°C/375°F and deep fry the cakes, a few at a time, until golden brown and puffy. Drain on absorbent kitchen paper.

4 Meanwhile, put all the syrup ingredients in a heavy saucepan and bring slowly to the boil, stirring. Simmer, stirring occasionally, for 20–30 minutes until the syrup thickens. Discard the cinnamon stick and serve the syrup with the bunuelos.

PREPARATION: 45 MINUTES
COOKING: 5 MINUTES
SERVES: 4–6

SOPAIPILLAS
Mexican fritters

1 Sift the flour, baking powder and salt into a bowl. Rub the fat into the flour and bind with enough lukewarm water to form a dough.

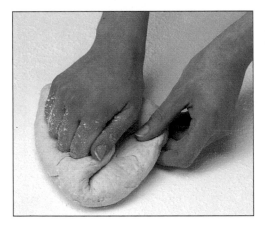

2 Knead the dough briefly until it is really smooth. Cover and then leave to stand at room temperature for about 20 minutes.

3 Roll out the dough on a lightly floured surface to 5mm/¼ inch thick. Cut the dough into 7.5cm/3 inch squares.

4 Heat the oil for deep frying to 200°C/400°F, and deep fry the pieces of dough, two or three at a time, until they are puffed up and golden. Turn once so that they are evenly coloured on both sides. Drain on absorbent kitchen paper. To serve, tear off a corner of each sopaipilla and pour in some honey flavoured with cinnamon. Serve sprinkled with pomegranate seeds.

250g/8oz flour
1 tablespoon baking powder
½ teaspoon salt
1 tablespoon lard
150-175ml/5-6 fl oz lukewarm water
oil for deep frying
honey warmed with a little ground cinnamon
To garnish:
fresh pomegranate seeds

PREPARATION: 35 MINUTES
COOKING: 5-10 MINUTES
SERVES: 4-6

CHURROS
Doughnuts

1 Cut the butter into pieces and put in a large saucepan with the water. Heat the water gently until the butter melts and then bring to a rolling boil.

3 Spoon the mixture into a piping bag fitted with a large star nozzle. Pipe it into 15cm/6 inch lengths, cutting between them. Heat the oil for deep frying in a large saucepan.

150g/5oz butter
300ml/½ pint water
150g/5oz flour
3 eggs
1 egg yolk
grated rind of 1 orange
vegetable oil for deep frying
1 tablespoon ground cinnamon
150g/5oz caster sugar

2 Sift the flour at least twice and, as soon as the water boils, tip it into the pan all at once. Remove from the heat and beat in the flour. Continue beating until the mixture forms a ball and leaves the sides of the pan clean. Cool a little and then beat in the eggs, the extra yolk and the orange rind.

PREPARATION: 20 MINUTES
COOKING: 10 MINUTES
SERVES: 4-6

4 Deep-fry the churros, a few at a time, until they are golden brown, turning them once. Remove and drain. Mix the cinnamon and sugar together and roll the churros in this mixture. Serve with some fresh fruit.

PAPAYAS Y PINA DIABLO

Papaya and pineapple flambé

1 Peel the papayas and scoop out the seeds. Cut the flesh into slices. Peel the pineapple and cut into thin slices. Remove the central core so that you are left with pineapple rings.

2 Melt the butter in a large heavy-based frying pan and then stir in the sugar over low heat, stirring until it is thoroughly dissolved. Add the lime juice and grated rind.

PREPARATION: 10 MINUTES
COOKING: 10 MINUTES
SERVES: 4–6

3 Increase the heat slightly and let the sugary mixture bubble for a few minutes until thickened. Take care that it does not burn or turn to caramel. Add the papaya and pineapple and cook gently for 2 minutes. Sprinkle with ground cinnamon.

2 papayas
1 small pineapple
50g/2oz butter
50g/2oz soft brown sugar
juice and grated rind of 1 lime
½ teaspoon ground cinnamon
4 tablespoons tequila
To decorate:
slivers of lime rind

4 Add the tequila to the pan, then stand well back and set it alight. When the flames die down, divide the flambéed papaya and pineapple between 4 serving dishes. Decorate with slivers of lime rind.

HELADO DE MANGO E PAPAYA

Swirled mango and papaya ice cream

250ml/8 fl oz milk

4 egg yolks

125g/4oz sugar

pinch of salt

250ml/8 fl oz fresh mango purée

1-2 teaspoons lime juice

250ml/8 fl oz double cream

150ml/5 fl oz fresh papaya purée

2 tablespoons white rum

icing sugar to taste

2 Pour the custard into a bowl and cool. Stir in the mango purée and lime juice. Whip the cream until thick and beat lightly into the mango mixture. Pour into a rigid container, cover and freeze until just firm.

3 Mix together the papaya purée and rum, and then sweeten to taste with some icing sugar.

4 Put alternate spoonfuls of mango ice cream and the papaya mixture into a freezeproof container, and stir gently with a spoon to make a swirled effect. Cover and return to the freezer until firm. Soften at room temperature before serving.

1 Scald the milk in a heavy saucepan. Lightly beat the egg yolks with the sugar and salt until the mixture is pale. Gradually stir in the hot milk, then return to the saucepan and cook over low heat, stirring until the custard thickens. Do not allow to boil or the custard will curdle.

PREPARATION: 20 MINUTES
FREEZING: 4-5 HOURS
SERVES: 6-8

CAPIROTADA
Mexican bread pudding

250ml/8 fl oz water

250g/8oz dark brown sugar

1½ teaspoons ground cinnamon

10 slices stale bread

50g/2oz butter

50g/2oz sultanas

125g/4oz walnuts, chopped

175g/6oz cottage cheese

2 Remove the crusts from the bread and cut into small cubes. Melt the butter in a large frying pan, add the bread cubes and fry gently until golden brown. Remove from the heat and stir in the syrup.

3 Add the sultanas, chopped walnuts and cottage cheese. Stir well and then simmer gently for a few minutes until all the ingredients are well blended.

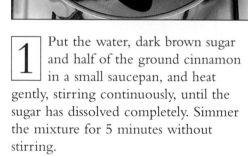

1 Put the water, dark brown sugar and half of the ground cinnamon in a small saucepan, and heat gently, stirring continuously, until the sugar has dissolved completely. Simmer the mixture for 5 minutes without stirring.

4 Transfer the mixture to a well-greased ovenproof dish and sprinkle with the remaining cinnamon. Cook in a preheated oven at 190°C/375°F/ Gas Mark 5 for 15-20 minutes until set and golden brown. Serve warm with cream.

PREPARATION: 20 MINUTES
COOKING: 15-20 MINUTES
SERVES: 4

TORTILLAS, SAUCES AND DRINKS

TORTILLAS
Corn tortillas

250g/8oz masa harina
175ml/6 fl oz water

Mix the masa harina and water together in a bowl with a fork to make a smooth dough. Add more water if necessary. Cover with a damp cloth and set aside for 15-20 minutes. Divide the dough into 12 portions and shape into balls. Flatten them in a tortilla press or by rolling them out with a rolling pin. Heat an ungreased griddle or cast-iron pan until it is very hot and cook the tortillas, one at a time, for 1½-2 minutes on each side until they are lightly browned. Gently press out any bubbles that form while they are cooking. Wrap the cooked tortillas in a cloth and serve warm in a basket. Alternatively, use them for making tacos, tostadas etc. This quantity of dough makes 12 tortillas. These are the traditional corn tortillas with a slightly heavier texture than the ones made with wheat flour.

SALSA VERDE FRESCA
Fresh green tomato and chilli sauce

300g/10oz canned tomatillos(Mexican green tomatoes), drained and chopped
1 small onion, finely chopped
1 garlic clove, crushed
2 fresh green chillies, seeded and finely chopped
salt and freshly ground black pepper
pinch of sugar
few sprigs fresh coriander, chopped

Put all the ingredients in a bowl and mix thoroughly until they are well blended. Alternatively, you can blend them together in a food processor or blender for a smoother sauce – if so, add some chopped green pepper to bulk it out. Serve the sauce with fish, meat and chicken dishes, moles and tacos.

SALSA ROJA
Red chilli sauce

5 small dried red chillies, crumbled
3 tablespoons boiling water
425g/14oz canned chopped tomatoes
4 tablespoons oil
2 onions, chopped
2 garlic cloves, crushed
3 tablespoons tomato paste
1 teaspoon ground cumin
1 teaspoon ground coriander
1½ tablespoons wine vinegar
1 teapoon sugar

Place the chillies and boiling water in a blender goblet or food processor. Drain the tomatoes, reserving the juice, and add the chopped tomatoes to the chillies. Blend until smooth and pour into a jug. Heat the oil in a small frying pan and sauté the onions and garlic until soft. Stir in the blended tomato mixture, the reserved tomato juice, tomato paste, cumin, coriander, vinegar and sugar. Cover and simmer for 10 minutes. Serve with tacos, enchiladas, meat, poultry and fish dishes.

SALSA DE JITOMATE
Tomato sauce

2 tablespoons olive oil
1 medium onion, finely chopped
1 garlic clove, crushed
4 large tomatoes, skinned and chopped
2 fresh green chillies, seeded and chopped
good pinch of sugar
salt and freshly ground black pepper
1 tablespoon chopped fresh coriander

Heat the oil in a saucepan and add the onion and garlic. Sauté until tender and lightly golden. Blend the tomatoes and chillies in a blender or food processor, and add to the onion mixture with the sugar, salt and plenty of ground black pepper. Simmer gently for about 15 minutes, stirring occasionally until thickened. Stir in the chopped coriander. Serve hot with meat and fish dishes.

SALSA CRUDA
Uncooked tomato chilli sauce

500g/1lb large ripe tomatoes, skinned and chopped
2 fresh green chillies, seeded and finely chopped
1 onion, finely chopped
pinch of sugar
salt and freshly ground black pepper
few sprigs fresh coriander, chopped

Put the tomatoes, chillies and onion in a bowl with the sugar. Season to taste and stir in the coriander.

CHILI CON QUESO
Chilli and cheese dip

2 tablespoons oil
75g/3oz chopped onion
2 garlic cloves, crushed
125g/4oz can green chillies, drained, seeded and chopped
3-4 tablespoons chopped seeded jalapeño chillies(optional)
250g/8oz tomatoes, skinned, seeded and chopped
75g/3oz cream cheese
250g/8oz Cheddar cheese, grated
salt

Heat the oil in a heavy saucepan, and add the onion and garlic. Cook gently, stirring occasionally, until softened. Add the chillies and tomatoes, and cook until any excess liquid has evaporated, stirring frequently. Add the cheeses and cook very gently over low heat, stirring the mixture until the cheeses have melted into the dipping sauce. Season to taste with salt. Serve warm as a dip.

CHOCOLATE MEXICANO
Mexican hot chocolate

600ml/1 pint milk
125g/4oz plain chocolate, grated
3 tablespoons sugar
1/2 teaspoon ground cinnamon
2-3 drops vanilla essence
pinch of ground cloves

Put the milk and grated chocolate in a medium-sized saucepan, and add the sugar, cinnamon, vanilla essence and cloves. Place the pan over moderate heat and stir constantly until the chocolate and milk are well blended and the sugar has dissolved. Bring to the boil, and then beat with a whisk or a traditional wooden molinillo(Mexican chocolate whisk) until frothy. Serve in cups or mugs sprinkled with a little ground cinnamon, if wished.

MARGARITA
Mexican tequila cocktail

2 tablespoons freshly squeezed lime juice
coarsely ground salt
2 tablespoons white tequila
1 tablespoon curacao or Triple Sec
ice cubes or crushed ice

Put 2 teaspoons of the lime juice in a shallow container and dip the rim of the cocktail glass in it. Next dip the rim of the glass into a saucer of coarsely ground salt. Mix the tequila with the curacao or Triple Sec and the remaining lime juice. Pour into the prepared glass and serve iced. Add a twist of lime peel if wished. **Note:** for an iced margarita, blend the tequila, lime juice and curacao or Triple Sec with plenty of crushed ice in a blender until slushy. Serve in the prepared frosted glass.

AGUA DE LIMON
Fresh lime or lemon drink

1 litre/1 2/3 pints water
125g/4oz sugar
1 whole lime or lemon
juice of 3 limes or lemons
ice cubes or crushed ice

Pour half the water into a blender with the sugar and 1 whole lime or lemon, quartered. Add the squeezed lime or lemon juice, and blend until thoroughly mixed and the lime or lemon peel has been whizzed into tiny green or yellow specks in the drink. Strain into a jug containing the remaining water and mix well. Serve with ice cubes or crushed ice and a twist of lime or lemon peel.

INDEX